Perfect Puppy Parent Guide

Discover the Secrets to Training any Puppy in just 21 Days, Even if You're a Clueless Beginner.

Written by Dorian Burton

PERFECT PUPPY PARENT

PERFECT PUPPY PARENT

© COPYRIGHT 2019 - ALL RIGHTS RESERVED.

The content contained within this book may not be reproduced, duplicated or transmitted without direct written permission from the author or the publisher.

Under no circumstances will any blame or legal responsibility be held against the publisher, or author, for any damages, reparation, or monetary loss due to the information contained within this book. Either directly or indirectly.

Legal Notice:

This book is copyright protected. This book is only for personal use. You cannot amend, distribute, sell, use, quote or paraphrase any part, or the content within this book, without the consent of the author or publisher.

Disclaimer Notice:

Please note the information contained within this document is for educational and entertainment purposes only. All effort has been executed to present accurate, up to date, and reliable, complete information. No warranties of any kind are declared or implied. Readers acknowledge that the author is not engaging in the rendering of legal, financial, medical or professional advice. The content within this book has been derived from various sources. Please consult a licensed professional before attempting any techniques outlined in this book.

By reading this document, the reader agrees that under no circumstances is the author responsible for any losses, direct or indirect, which are incurred as a result of the use of the information contained within this document, including, but not limited to, — errors, omissions, or inaccuracies.

TABLE OF CONTENTS

1   Introduction   1

2   5 Most Popular Dog Training Methods, and Which is Right for You and Your Puppy   6

3   3 Essential Training Skills That Your Puppy Needs + Things You NEED to Know Beforehand   15

4   Powerful Potty Training for First Time Puppy Owners   24

5   5 Essential Commands Your Puppy Needs to Know   30

6   Conclusion   34

7   Resources   37

PERFECT PUPPY PARENT

INTRODUCTION

A dog is a man's best friend. It comes as no surprise to me that you have decided to add one to your family. They are one of the best pets you can ever have. I am speaking from experience because I have three. Surprisingly, they are also the easiest to train when you know what you are doing. No one wants a dog that is disobedient and does not listen to even your most basic commands.

You want a best friend that is easy to control so that you can take them with you everywhere you go, without having to worry about a catastrophe occurring around every corner. Luckily for you, I am here to help! My goal is simple, and its to enable and empower you be able to train your own puppy.

I will show you how to take your puppy from a blank slate to a fully trained and well-behaved puppy in less than 30 days. If you have had your new puppy for a few days, then surely you have already discovered that they have some bad habits, like going to the bathroom in your living room and barking non-stop throughout the night.

I am here to help you eliminate all those issues in no time! But first, let me introduce myself properly. My name is Dorian Burton, and over the years as a dog trainer, I've trained hundreds of dogs of all different breeds and sizes. It doesn't matter if you have a Great Dane or a Teacup Yorkshire Terrier - they can all be trained with the right guidance.

I know it might seem like a strange job, but working with and training dogs is my passion and what I love to do. Being that my parents were avid dog lovers, I have always been around dogs since the day I was born. Dogs stole my heart from a very young age, and they will surely steal yours, too.

Earlier, I mentioned that I have three dogs of my own. My love for my 3 babies Moxie (Boxer), Bailey (Husky), and Rocket (Border collie) is what inspired me to turn my passion into my career. I started off by training my babies, and from then on I couldn't help myself. It was all I wanted to do after that!

I want to show people that, with a little bit of training, dogs really are a man's best friend. Through training, you create a bond between you and your dog, as well as mutual respect, which is the core of any relationship. It also creates a form of trust, because if your dog does not trust you, you can't trust your dog to listen to your commands.

Once you have taken your puppy through proper

training, you will have a little pup that you can take anywhere and be proud of. Like I mentioned before, trust and respect are core characteristics of a strong relationship with your dog. To do this, you need to be able to train your puppy the right way from a young age. After you do that, you will have a loyal and dedicated doggy sidekick for life!

Training your dog is not a one-way relationship. It takes work and dedication from your side to ensure that your dog knows what you want and that you make your instructions as clear as possible to them. People thank me for how my training has changed their lives and helped them build a deeper and more meaningful relationship with their dog.

This is the exact same training that I will be unveiling in this book - training that is easy for anyone to get results with. It does not have to be hard; anyone can do it! I have taught children from as young as 10 years old.

With my help and expertise, you will be fully equipped with the skills and knowledge you need to be able to take your puppy from a naughty little troublemaker to an obedient and loyal canine companion - a puppy that you can entertain your family and friends with. Some have even gone as far as teaching their dogs to dance and perform on stage. The stronger your bond, the easier it will become to teach your pup new tricks.

Have you ever heard the saying "old habits die hard?" Well... this is very true, especially when it comes to training your dog. Your puppy's brain acts like a sponge. They soak up all the information that is provided to them.

Over time, their brain will fill up and new habits and skills will become harder to learn. So, it is very important to train your puppy as early and young as possible, or you will miss out on the most valuable time to train your dog. You know the saying "old dogs can't learn new tricks?" This is not entirely true, but it is crucial that you do not wait around to train your puppy.

The older they are, the more difficult it will be to train them properly without fail. As mentioned, their brains do eventually fill up and it becomes harder to teach them, but not impossible. It just takes some harder work and more dedication than it would with a 12-week-old puppy.

The puppy training tips and tricks that you're about to read are proven to yield incredible results for puppies of all ages, breeds, and sizes. It is remarkable to see how fast they learn and how easy it becomes for their owners to teach them new things and discipline them in a manner that isn't harmful.

Every chapter in this book will provide you with actionable steps that will help you to get rid of your puppy's undesirable habits and instill good behaviors and doggy qualities so you can take your dog anywhere and show them off to the world.

If you follow the training in this book step by step and understand what you are reading, it is very likely that you will never have to train your puppy ever again.

This book is designed to be a quick read for you to

understand a good foundation of how dog training works, and how we use their nature to train them effectively.

So, let's get started!

5 Most Popular Dog Training Methods, and Which is Right for You and Your Puppy

There are millions of web pages on the internet filled with loads of information on how you can train your dog. When I was just starting out, this is what frustrated me the most. I had to filter through hundreds of documents before I could find exactly what I was looking for.

I spent so much time on the internet and reading books that I started losing my connection to the outside world, just by trying to understand what was best for me and my best friend. Time is valuable to many people, and to your pets. They do not live forever, as much as we wish they did.

To make things as easy on you and your dog as I possibly can, I am going to briefly tell you about 5 of the most popular dog training methods. Some work better than others, but in the end, they are all highly effective training methods. In this book, I'll be showing you how to train your puppy with my favorite of these methods, but we'll talk more about that later. Now let's get into it.

5 Popular Dog training methods

1. Positive reinforcement

Positive reinforcement is stated as number one on my list because this is by far the best option for both you and your dog. This method has proven to be successful with all types of breeds of the canine species. All things considered, positive reinforcement is the most effective and most straightforward method to teach to complete beginners and first-time puppy owners.

What is positive reinforcement? This method of training is very simple. If your dog does something you want them to and follows your command, you give them a treat immediately after they have completed the task at hand. This will show them and teach them that if they listen, they get rewarded.

Why does this method work? They will see this as a good thing and their behavior will start to change simply because they want their treat or toy more often! It is inevitable - dogs will repeat appropriate behavior when a reward is offered.

Make sure your commands are simple, like "sit" and "no." This method is also a great way to establish a good relationship with your dog, as it also helps a lot with communication. You will see the results if you are doing this correctly.

Remember that you do not want to scream or

shout at your dog when they misbehave, because they do not understand what you want or what you are saying. This will only cause your dog to develop anxiety when you are around, so do not punish them by spanking them with a newspaper or your hands.

Eventually, you can start moving away from treats and reward them with a nice pat on the head and scratching behind the ears, but this is only when they start understanding the reward system you have set in place and only when it starts becoming effective.

If you are living alone this will be easy, because it needs to be reinforced consistently. If you have others in the house, tell them about the reward system. Be sure not to overfeed when rewarding, and try and be patient when it comes to flushing away the bad behavior by not giving treats and toys or petting sessions.

2. Alpha dog or dominance

When we look at the history of dogs, we know that they form packs and families with a dominant alpha of the pack. This method works with that same idea, that dogs develop dominant and submissive relationships within their packs. Dogs usually fight for dominance when it comes to establishing hierarchy. This works the same way with humans when dogs see themselves as the alpha over you or other family members.

What is the alpha dog method, exactly? This

method of training is basically showing the dog that you are the alpha in your home. This includes getting down on your knees and making eye contact with your pet and not allowing them on any of your furniture.

Why does this method work? You can get this right by showing dominance and projecting confidence and authority. This will show the dog that you are in charge and they will start submitting and listening to what you are saying. You also need to understand the body language of your dog to perfect this technique.

Some studies have shown that things have changed when it comes to a dog's instincts so this method may bring on bad behavior and anxiety around you and your dog if this is not implemented in a pleasant way.

Many trainers use this method along with a few other methods of training to get it to function at its full potential. This training also needs consistency in order to work, which can make it difficult for children and senior citizens.

3. Scientific training

This one has proven to be more difficult, as everything around us is changing and evolving every second of the day. Scientific training solely relies on information about your dog, the effectiveness of punishment and rewards, their nature, and how they are conditioned. With information changing quickly, it becomes hard to define scientific training.

To understand your dog, you need to know what type of breed it is, what they can and can't eat, why they behave the way they do, and look for any warning signs of a temper and what will trigger bad behavior from them.

Scientific training, at its core, is about understanding your dog in every way you can by analyzing their behavior to form an off-leash bond between you and your pup. This will often go hand in hand with other methods like positive reinforcement and minimizing punishment as often as you can.

Why does this method work? This method works because you will have a better understanding of your dog and their behavior, which allow you to build a better communication system.

If you implement this along with other training methods, it can be very effective for both you and your companion. It can become difficult, though, as things change over time and you need to monitor the situation and behaviors as often as you can to keep up to date with the psychology of your dog.

4. Clicker training

This form of training is more common than anything that I have seen before, mainly because it goes well with positive reinforcement. This works with the exact same principles of positive reinforcement, only with a small device that makes a sharp noise or a click.

You can buy these almost anywhere. I got mine from a local pet shop, and they are not expensive at all. I have personally used this method on my own dogs and it works wonders, especially if you are just starting out.

What is clicker training? This method uses a device called a clicker that makes a noise to show your dog that they have completed what you wanted them to. This is always followed by a treat for a job well done. This goes well with positive reinforcement, so remember to praise them, too.

Why does this method work? As stated with positive reinforcement, clicker training works because your puppy will begin to associate the action with positivity. It will teach them that when they hear a click or a sharp sound, they will be receiving a treat for completing the task. Being given treats often encourages positive behavior.

This method is also used for teaching dogs tricks and new commands, but first, the dog needs to be taught that a click or noise means he or she is going to get a treat now. There are many ways to do this. For example, you can tell them to sit, and when they do click your clicker and give them a treat.

5. Electronic training

This last one does not focus on the good that your dog does, but the bad. Electronic training refers to a collar that is placed on your dog, and when they do something bad it releases a shot of citronella or a small electric shock to your dog.

This training is mostly used when your dog is at a distance and not on a leash. This could be to keep a dog in your yard if it jumps over your walls. Please note that this type of training is not for beginners, but professionals only, because if you do not know what you are doing you can cause a lot of damage to your dog's health.

If you are going to try it, consult a professional to find out how to use these devices, because if you do not you can cause permanent anxiety in your dog.

There are many reasons as to why most people do not use this method of training. The main reason is that it is basically a form of punishment and there is no positive reinforcement. So, your dog does not get positive reinforcement with this technique, which means even if they do something right, they do not get rewarded. They only get punished if they do something wrong.

I don't recommend electronic training to beginners. There are many other ways to train your dog - ways that put them under much less stress.

Dog psychology

Just to make it clear, my favorite method of training is positive reinforcement. This method is what this book is going to be about. Not to say that the other methods do not work too - they all work - but this is how I train my dogs and it works perfectly each and every time.

Now let's jump into the psyche of man's best friend. No one really knows how dogs became domesticated, but there are theories out there that say that they self-domesticated. Dogs are highly intelligent so I will proceed with that theory.

Dogs have problem-solving skills and the ability to process information in their own way to be able to understand us and our body language. They also have a very sharp sense of smell and acute vision as well as a remarkable sense of hearing. Additionally, they are sensitive to the Earth's magnetic fields. All of these senses contribute to their ability to "read" humans. They can read our facial expressions, body posture, and even hand signals. Dogs are even empathetic to human beings, and they can understand when we are in pain.

My dogs each have a personality of their own, all dogs do. Dogs each have different personalities and react to things differently than one another. Some come off as aggressive and some playful, some are scared of lightning and others of people.

This is why it is important to teach your pup properly from a young age. If you beat them all the time, it is going to cause aggression and anxiety as well as possessiveness. This is why I always lean towards positive reinforcement when training.

Loving and playing with your dog has proven to release hormones that make them happy, and therefore they will seek to do whatever they did to please you more often. If you praise them, they are smart enough to know that they are doing something right and will, therefore, repeat their behavior.

This is why it is best to train your dog with methods like positive reinforcement and clicker training. They are smart enough to process the click as "hey, I am going to get food now" and understanding and knowing how your dog works will be a benefit to you and your dog.

With training, we try to eliminate anything that will lead to snapping or irritability. Most of all, we do not want our pets to start randomly attacking us or other people. You need to know that you have to pick up on the small signs that your dog has a problem so that you can solve the problem before it gets too serious.

It is also important to note that all dogs are different, just like I am not exactly like my parents or my siblings. That is why a puppy's response to training will be different with each puppy, but positive reinforcement is the kind of training that most puppies will react to the best.

3 Essential Training Skills That Your Puppy Needs + Things You NEED to Know Beforehand

The first thing you need to know before you get a dog is that when you get a dog, it is not a short-term commitment. A dog is essentially a lifelong commitment. Whether it's your entire life, or your dogs. If you can imagine yourself having a dog for a year and then deciding to get rid of them because they aren't cute anymore or because they are getting old, then you are far from ready to get one.

A dog is like a child. You can't get rid of them when they annoy you or ignore them because the excitement is gone. There are so many dogs in shelters and many being put down because their families gave up on them, so be sure that you are ready for this.

A dog needs fresh food and water every single day, because food will become stale and when dogs drink water, they leave a snotty layer at the bottom of the bowl. If you clean out their bowls every day you will know what I am talking about! They need fresh food and water without fail, or they will become sick.

A dog also needs to be groomed and bathed often

to prevent fleas and matted hair, and for their general well-being, especially if they are going to live inside your house. Another thing you need to get is tick and flea shampoo, because dogs need to get exercise and when they play in the grass or in a park, they will can pick up fleas and ticks.

And it is my opinion, but you HAVE to make sure that your pup gets vaccinated against all the possible diseases that are out there. You need to make sure this is done on time and regularly. You do not want your pup to get sick or die because you did not vaccinate them.

Like I mentioned before, many dogs end up in shelters, so be sure to make an appointment with your vet to spay or neuter your dog while they are still young. For male dogs, this will prevent them from marking their territory everywhere they go. From what I have seen, if you get your females fixed, they tend to be more relaxed and you will not have to clean blood off your floor when they are in heat.

One last thing you need to know is if you are buying your dog from a breeder, you should probably know that the puppy needs to stay with its mother for a minimum of 8 weeks. This is very important, because the mother's milk is what will keep them strong and prevent things like separation anxiety. Make sure that the breeder gets the first round of shots done as well.

When you do eventually get your pup, the first thing you need to do is call the vet and make an appointment for a general check-up. This is for your own piece of mind to ensure your pup is 100% healthy, as well as establish a rapport with a local vet that will be there for you and your puppy in the long run.

3 Essential Training Skills that Your Puppy Needs

I am not going to go into a lot of detail just yet, but there are 3 essential training skills that your puppy needs to know in order to be a well-trained puppy. We will go into each one in detail in the next few chapters. These essential training skills are:

1. Crate training
2. Potty training
3. Common commands

The most common commands that your dog must know are "sit," "down," "come," "stay," and "no."

Before you start training your dog, there are a few things you need to know. Firstly, it is never okay to harshly punish your dog, no matter what their behavior is. Things will get frustrating, but that is no excuse to take out your frustrations on your pet.

No one said that training a dog would be easy. They have very short attention spans in the beginning; therefore, you need to make learning sessions as short and simple as possible. Remember that using force will not help you in the situation. You need to show your dog what you want them to know in order for them to understand what you want.

Make sure that your house is a safe place for your dog so that they feel at ease where they are. This will be the place where you will be making your training routine become a daily habit. Make sure that your dog is comfortable in their safe place before deciding to make it a public routine.

If you start training in public, this could cause your dog to get anxiety. They will never learn like this due to all the distractions. There will be too many eyes and ears and smells for your dog to concentrate on the task at hand. This is why I recommend that you only take them out publicly once your training is successful and completed.

Remember, you need to always use positive reinforcement when training your dog. Please do not push your dog very hard at the start, because they are still learning. Your aim is to make the training for both of you as fun and entertaining as possible, so also try to keep yourself in the training exercises as well. No one likes to do things alone.

During training, make sure that you are in a quiet environment to avoid any distractions. This will help with your training immensely. Remember to reward your puppy for a job well done each and every single time. This is where positive reinforcement comes in. Remember to praise them, too, so that they understand that they have made you happy and they know you are about to give them a treat.

Do note that your dog is still new to this, so please

remember to be as patient as you can and train regularly. Once your dog properly learns a command, then you can start teaching him or her new ones. Take baby steps and do not try to throw everything at them all at once. This will just confuse them, and you will have to start all over again.

If you do not live alone, make sure that every member of your family gets a chance to train your dog. This way if you are gone for any length of time, your family can still continue the training schedule with your dog. Your puppy will also be able to train with every member of your family without a problem, and thus form a bond with everyone.

General questions asked by first-time puppy owners.

You probably have a lot of questions. I am here to answer some of the most common questions asked when it comes to getting a new dog. Feel free to skip around to the information you need the most.

At what age can I start training my puppy?

You should be training your puppy the second they get home to make sure your puppy learns the correct discipline from a very young age. This could be done as young as 7 to 8 weeks of age. If you are buying your dog from a breeder, the breeder may have already started with the basics, such as socialization and communication. Some breeders will even house train puppies before they go to their new homes!

What is food lure training?

This is a trick to teach your puppy to sit (or any other command, really) by moving a piece of food to where you want them to be. For example, if you want to get your puppy to sit down, you should slowly hold the food up over the puppy's nose and move slightly back. This should get you a sitting down response. This is food lure training in practice, and it is very easy to do.

Food lure training will go hand in hand with positive reinforcement training. This will teach your dog that if they complete a task, they will get praise, pets, and treats. This is crucial for the first few days you are training your dog, until they get the hang of it. I believe that food lure training is necessary for the beginning of positive reinforcement training.

How much time should I spend training my puppy every day?

The simple answer is, in the beginning, a short 5-minute session once a day is ideal. Once your dog is used to these shorter sessions, you can go for 15 minutes of training every day, breaking it up into three times a day (so 5 minutes each). Remember to praise your dog after he completes a task.

How do I keep my puppy from becoming distracted during training?

You need to keep your dog in a controlled and quiet environment, which will help to minimize distractions. Also, hold off on feeding times until you are ready to train your dog. This will show them that if they focus and concentrate on their training, they will get food. When a dog is hungry, they tend to pay more attention to the food that you will be holding in your hand.

When is it safe to take my dog out in public?

You should only take your dog out once they have been fully vaccinated to protect them against diseases. You do not have to take your puppy to a public place to train them. Socialization with other dogs is important, but ensure you are keeping your pup's safety in mind at all times. You do not want your best friend to pick up the deadly parvovirus.

What can I expect on mine and my pup's first visit to the vet?

The vet will check your dog's immune system and stool. They will look for things like parasites, diseases, and anything that might be life-threatening to your dog. If your dog is healthy, you can start training immediately. If you've acquired your puppy from a breeder, they should have records of vaccinations, vet visits, and the medical history of the mother.

What shots does my puppy need, and how often do they need them?

Your puppy needs 3 sets of shots. The first shots are given when they are between 7 and 8 weeks of age. This will protect them against 5 separate diseases, such as parvovirus, hepatitis, distemper, parainfluenza, and leptospirosis.

These 5 separate diseases will be covered with each set of shots. You need to ensure that your dog has their shots every 3 weeks from their very first shot. After the age of 16 weeks, they will be given a rabies shot. After the rabies shot, they will need another shot once every year in order to maintain their immunity.

What type of food should I give my dog?

Each dog is different. You need to test which one will suit your puppy best. Some dogs will be allergic to one type of food, and others will be able to eat anything. This should go without saying, but you need to feed your dog puppy food specifically for the first year of their life, otherwise they may develop digestive problems and they will not be able to get the proper nutrition they need to grow big and strong. You need to be sure that at the bottom of the packet it is recommended by a veterinarian and has a lot of protein, fat, vitamins, and minerals. After 12 months, you can start moving to adult food.

My puppy had an accident on my carpets. How do I get the smell out?

You need to act quickly! Grab an old towel or sponge of any sort, go to the area where your dog had their accident, and soak up the liquid in the carpet. Next, wet the carpet with cold water as thoroughly as you can and soak that up, too. Then, find a product that will remove the odor from your carpets. I simply use Dettol. I usually leave it for 6-7 minutes, then soak up the remaining liquid. Allow it to dry thoroughly. You might need to repeat these steps more than once.

Powerful Potty Training for First Time Puppy Owners

If you are aiming to have an inside dog, this chapter is the most important for you. I think it goes without saying that your dog needs to be potty trained for it to live in or even be in your house. There are a few things that you need to know before you start potty training your puppy.

When your pup first has an accident, you need to clean up with an enzymatic cleaner to minimize odors that might attract your dog back to relieve themselves in the same place. With this being said, you need to stay away from ammonia-based cleaners, because this will encourage your dog to go relieve itself on the same place.

It is never okay for any reason to punish your puppy for having an accident in your house. As mentioned before, this will teach them to fear you and they will develop anxiety. We don't want your best friend to be afraid of you, so remember that positive reinforcement is always the key.

If you do happen to stumble upon an accident, do not scream, yell at, or hit your dog. Do not take their face and rub their nose in it. They will not know what they are being punished for. Remember, your aim is not to punish your dog at all.

You need to constantly use positive reinforcement for them to understand what they are doing right as opposed to what they're doing wrong. They will also take your anger and process that into fear of you because they don't know what they have done wrong.

If you happen to catch them in the act, loudly clap your hands to draw their attention so that they know they have done something that they were not supposed to do. Then gently take them outside by calling them or tugging lightly on their collar and let them finish outside.

Once your dog has completed its business, remember to praise them and give them a treat. This will show them that if they do their business outside of your house, they will get a treat and pets. While in training, it would be better for you to take your puppy out and give them some time to sniff around and get to know their environment.

You need to stay outside with your puppy to make sure that they relieve themselves. You can avoid accidents this way. It is also important to note that it can take months for a puppy to become fully house trained.

Like I mentioned before, not every dog is the same. So, this time will vary between breed, size, and personality of your dog.

Now, you are probably wondering when the right time would be to start potty training your puppy. You can start anywhere between 12 weeks and 16 weeks old, because studies have shown that they have enough control of their bladder and bowel to learn how to hold it like we humans do.

How do I know that my puppy needs to go? You need to know that if your dog is in a small confined space such as a crate, if they start digging or whining these are signs that you need to take them out because it's time for them to go and do their business.

If they are not confined to a small space, look for things like barking, scratching, circling and sniffing around. These are all signs that your dog needs to go, and you should not wait. So, take him outside and don't forget the treats.

If you are a small breed pet owner, you probably want to housebreak your dog in your house using pee pads as their place to go or a specially designed crate that looks like a sheet of grass. House potty breaking methods should be up to you and how you choose to do it.

For indoor dogs, it's easy to define a small place where they will be allowed to go and do their business, but putting the crate there alone is not going to teach your dog to go when it needs to go. He still needs to be taught that that is the only place they will be allowed to go.

When do I take my dog out? You need to take your dog out after they eat or drink anything, first thing in the morning, at night before bed, after playing indoors or chewing up a toy, and after spending time in a crate or waking up from a nap.

Also, something to take note of, if your dog is fully house trained and starts defecating and relieving itself in your home, these could be signs of a medical problem. You should get your dog to a vet if they start doing this. This could be a sign of a urinary tract infection, among other things.

Begin to train your pup.

1. Taking Control

When first training your puppy, taking control is important. Taking control means that you will show them where they are allowed to do their business and where not. For short term use, crate training would be the best for this period. This way, you will get to know your dog and when your dog needs to go.

Many people will start off with confinement by either using a leash or, as mentioned above, the crate method. I know it's impossible to keep track of your dog for 24 hours a day, 7 days a week. This is why it will be ideal to start confining them in a small place to learn bladder control. If you want to train your dog indoors, maybe you should consider getting puppy gates.

The idea of this is to get your dog used to a small confined space where they are comfortable. They will choose not to go or relieve themselves in that specific area. If this is done correctly, you will be able to see that there will be a decrease in potty accidents and a major increase in bladder control.

2. Meal times and routine

Do not free feed your dog. This means that you do not leave food out all day for the puppy to eat freely. You can set meal plan times and remove the food once they are done eating. This way, you can easily establish their potty times.

The next thing you need to do is set up a routine word for going potty. This could be anything from a phrase to a word or a gesture. If you want to train your dog to be an outdoor dog, you need to teach them to either sit in front of the door when they need to go out, or sit at the door and bark once.

This can be switched and changed around at any time, as long as you've established that when they need to go, they are able to alert you about it.

3. Set your potty area

By setting a potty area when it comes to outdoor dogs, it's easy for you to fence off a place where you would like them to do their business and make it their place only. If you are planning to have your dog indoors, make sure that the crate that you have for them is there at all times and that it's easily accessible.

Once you have set your potty area, your dog will then learn to alert you when he needs to go. This is when you take them to their designated area where they can do their business. Be sure to have treats on hand so that as soon as they finish what they are doing, you can immediately treat them.

You are going to need to go with your dog each and every time until they are successfully potty trained. This means spending a little bit more extended time outside with your dog until they have finished the action so that you can reward them immediately after.

This also means that once they are ready to do this on their own, they will be able to give a signal for you to open the door or they will walk to their crate indoors to do their business. When you first start out with this, you need to be sure that you take them to the very same spot, as this will help them learn the routine.

5 Essential Commands Your Puppy Needs to Know

These are the five essentials your dog needs to know to maintain good behavior around you and your family and friends. They are simple to teach using positive reinforcement. You can find more information about this training in an earlier chapter.

1. Sit

Sit can be used for many different reasons: before food, for traveling, and pretty much anything that you need to get your dog to sit for. Teaching your dog how to sit on command is a sign of a well-behaved pooch.

You need to hold a treat close to the puppy's nose and start moving your hand behind their head slowly. This will put them in the sit position, and you should give them the treat after saying "sit." Keep in mind that this doesn't usually work the first time. You can encourage them into the sit position with light pressure on their rump, but don't force them down. If they try to turn or back up to get to the treat, try this method in a corner first so that they have less space to backup.

2. Down (as in lay down)

This one comes in handy when you have guests over and your dog decides to jump all over them. The down command is great for this and will show your guests that you have control over your dog, so they don't have anything to fear when you are near.

To teach your dog this trick, you need to show your dog that you have a treat and move it down to the floor. Your dog's nose will follow. Then, you should take the treat and move a few paces back until the dog is on its belly. Then say "down" and treat your dog for a job well done.

3. Come

This is probably is the easiest thing to teach your dog, especially if your dog likes to follow you around all day. Come is useful for this exact reason. If you want your dog to follow you around or find you when you need them, you need to teach them the command come. Considering dogs are naturally curious, this command should come easier.

If you need to put a collar on your dog, then do that and add a leash. Tug gently and say "come." When the dog gets to you, give him a treat. Eventually, remove the leash and practice without anything attaching the two of you. Move to progressively more distant locations, and at some point try calling them into a different room. You should also (slowly) add distractions to ensure they will come even when something else might be drawing their attention.

4. Stay

Stay is useful if you would like to leave your house. This command comes in handy in many other situations as well. Teaching your dog this command will be easy if your dog has learned previous commands. Remember, positive reinforcement and patience are key.

To get this right at first, you need to tell your dog to sit. Then say "stay" and move a few paces back. If they stay, reward them, and as time goes on you can take more steps back.

5. No

To teach your dog this command will be your most grateful asset, especially if your dog is destructive to furniture. To get the attention of your dog, clap loudly and say no. Whatever is in your dog's mouth will surely drop to the floor.

Once you have completed all of these, you can rest assured that you will have a well-trained dog. These commands can be taught within 21 days if the correct procedure is followed. Sometimes even less!

PERFECT PUPPY PARENT

CONCLUSION

Getting a dog is a wonderful experience. Learning to train them and then actually getting it right is very gratifying. It creates an unbreakable bond between you and your dog. It teaches respect and understanding - for both of you.

Through all of the training I have provided above, you will see that by the end of this book, not only did you successfully train your puppy, but you have created everlasting memories between you and your best friend. You should be proud of both yourself and your pup for getting to this point. They say that knowledge and power are the keys to success, and hopefully the knowledge in this book has provided you with some small measure of training success. I am glad you chose me to help you through this. I am proud of you, too!

Keep in mind that this book is not intended to be an exhaustive, detailed guide of every aspect of training. There's always more to learn! With the solid, foundational knowledge you've gained, you and your pup can go on to new heights. The five basic commands are just that - basic. Once you and your puppy have mastered them, there's almost no limit to what you can learn from there.

When you first decided to get a dog, you probably had 100 questions on how to take care of it and how you would train it. I am very glad to have provided this information to you and I am glad I could make it the slightest bit easier for you, as I have with my other clients that I have worked with.

I started writing books like this so that my readers could take some understanding of their dogs away from this book and have it for a lifetime. I wanted readers just like you to walk away feeling stress-free knowing what they needed to do as soon as their new dog walked into their home.

But most of all, I am glad that I could have walked this journey with you, knowing that everything you are doing for your dog is out of love. Thank you for all your patience, and I can't wait to hear how your dog has progressed on the way to its bright new future in your family!

Resources

5 Essential Commands You Can Teach Your Dog | Cesar's Way. (2019, April 9). Retrieved April 22, 2019, from https://www.cesarsway.com/5-essential-commands-you-can-teach-your-dog/

The 7 Most Important Dog Training Skills. (2019, April 15). Retrieved April 22, 2019, from https://www.rover.com/blog/important-dog-training-skills/

7 Most Popular Dog Training Methods - Dogtime. (2019, January 10). Retrieved April 22, 2019, from https://dogtime.com/reference/dog-training/50743-7-popular-dog-training-methods

10 Best Training Tips. (2016, October 19). Retrieved April 22, 2019, from https://www.pedigree.com/dog-care/training/10-best-training-tips

10 Frequently Asked Questions About Puppies. (n.d.). Retrieved April 22, 2019, from http://www.vetstreet.com/our-pet-experts/answers-to-10-of-the-most-common-questions-people-have-about-owning-a-new-puppy

The 10 Most Popular -- and Most Important -- Dog Training Cues. (2016, March 9). Retrieved April 22, 2019, from https://www.dogster.com/lifestyle/the-10-most-popular-and-most-important-dog-training-cues

15 Essential Commands to teach Your Dog. (2018b, December 27). Retrieved April 22, 2019, from https://www.insidedogsworld.com/essential-commands-to-teach-your-dog/

Crate training 101. (n.d.). Retrieved April 22, 2019, from https://www.humanesociety.org/resources/crate-training-101

Crate Training a Puppy: How to Potty Train Your Dog. (n.d.). Retrieved April 22, 2019, from https://www.akc.org/expert-advice/training/how-to-crate-train-a-puppy/

Five Basic Obedience Commands Your Dog Should Learn. (n.d.). Retrieved April 22, 2019, from https://www.southbostonanimalhospital.com/blog/five-basic-obedience-commands-your-dog-should-learn

House Training Your Puppy. (2009, December 16). Retrieved April 22, 2019, from https://pets.webmd.com/dogs/guide/house-training-your-puppy

How To Crate Train Your Dog » PAWS. (n.d.). Retrieved April 22, 2019, from https://www.paws.org/library/dogs/training/how-to-crate-train-your-dog/

Puppy Behavior and Training - Training Basics. (n.d.).

Retrieved April 22, 2019, from https://vcahospitals.com/know-your-pet/puppy-behavior-and-training-training-basics

Puppy Command Training | Purina. (2018, October 4). Retrieved April 22, 2019, from https://www.purina.com/articles/puppy/training/puppy-command-training

Puppy FAQs - The Answers You've Been Looking For. (n.d.). Retrieved April 22, 2019, from https://www.fidosavvy.com/puppy-faqs.html

Potty Training a Puppy: How to House Train Puppies. (n.d.). Retrieved April 22, 2019, from https://www.akc.org/expert-advice/training/how-to-potty-train-a-puppy/

Puppy Training FAQ - Ultimate Puppy. (2016, March 26). Retrieved April 22, 2019, from https://www.ultimatepuppy.com/puppy-training-faq/

Teach Your Puppy These 5 Basic Commands. (n.d.). Retrieved April 22, 2019, from https://www.akc.org/expert-advice/training/teach-your-puppy-these-5-basic-commands/

Top Ten Dog Training Tips | Petfinder. (n.d.). Retrieved April 22, 2019, from https://www.petfinder.com/dogs/dog-training/dog-training-tips/

PERFECT PUPPY PARENT

www.ingramcontent.com/pod-product-compliance
Lightning Source LLC
Chambersburg PA
CBHW030135100526
44591CB00009B/667